Against Institutions

Against Institutions

A Critique of Institutions

JOEL STEELE

WIPF & STOCK · Eugene, Oregon

AGAINST INSTITUTIONS
A Critique of Institutions

Wipf & Stock
An Imprint of Wipf and Stock Publishers
199 W. 8th Ave., Suite 3
Eugene, OR 97401

www.wipfandstock.com

PAPERBACK ISBN: 979-8-3852-3564-3
HARDCOVER ISBN: 979-8-3852-3565-0
EBOOK ISBN: 979-8-3852-3566-7

VERSION NUMBER 11/03/25

If a man objects to truths that are all too evident,
it is no easy task to find arguments that will change
his mind.

—EPICTETUS

Contents

Preface

This work addresses institutionalized societies and how institutions are far more detrimental to them than beneficial. It evaluates the government's self-prescribed role and its designated purpose. Included are monumental events that have resulted in significant shifts within the framework of these societies. Propaganda from revolutionary moments in history that fostered these social changes is discussed. The primary argument is against centrally planned systems of government. It exposes the impossibility of centrally planned ideologies in achieving the long sought-after utopian society. It examines why Keynesian theory is so widely accepted, particularly by governments. A comparative approach is used to illustrate the disconnect between relative production and aggregate demand. The theoretical structure developed by classical economists is applied to modern economic calamities, which was initiated by the unprecedented government intervention in 2020. The philosophy of history is employed to illustrate connections between political philosophy, academia, and institutions. Emerging from these critiques is a reality that the citizens of Western nations must confront their institutions and the ruling class that designed them.

Introduction

What is history but a fable agreed upon?

—Napoleon

The phrase above, attributed to Napoleon, questions the legitimacy of recorded history. If the victors write history, why wouldn't we expect narratives to be biased? Myth is often more important than reality since nearly all civilizations have formed their identity from myths. The contemporary view of history in academic institutions has been regarded as a culmination of errors. Tradition has been replaced by ideological factors that were designed to flush out global equality. Universities are no longer producing graduates who apply logic and reason to evaluate social events in history. The philosophies and accomplishments of Western civilizations no longer humble students. Students are more interested in sharing the knowledge they have amassed from social media and popular influencers in their short lives. Institutions encourage this behavior, not just because it assists in the overall systematic goal of social engineering but because there is a fear that any rebuke may result in damaging an already fragile ego. Contemporary generations are so sensitive that the slightest distress, initiated by a sociopolitical discussion, usually results in severe anxiety or even a mental breakdown. This is especially problematic if students are asked to entertain a different view than the one ingrained into their psyche via the public education system. To protect students, professors initiate talking points from approved media and political sources. Typically, they discuss the White Anglo-Saxon Patriarchy (WASP) and their exploitation and enslavement of other civilizations and races. Educational institutions do not provide a balanced approach when it comes to social history. In the academy, the primary focus is on the errors occurring in each stage of social development. These errors, academics argue, stem from colonialism and the aspirations of European conquest. This has resulted in blind resentment because there is no serious analysis regarding the justification of the cause according to social norms at any given time in history.[1] Politicians and political activists understand that ideology is controlled within the nation's institutions. The institutions have produced an apathetic, callow, and docile subject of the state. The product of these institutions has contributed to the decline of the West. If the West is not in decline, it is at least in a state of disarray brought on by arbitrary social experiments via state-affiliated institutions. This treatise critiques the institutionalization of societies and argues for a return to a classical government articulated by Aristotle in his *Politics*.

---

1. My experience working for a large evangelical university while collecting data for this research.

I

Centralized Planning

Those born in the United States who have been US citizens their entire lives will retain certain events and ideologies that shaped American history. A broad overview of the government's designated purpose in society serves as a reminder of narrowly focused, monumental events that caused societal shifts. In his publication *Common Sense*, Thomas Paine wrote, "Society is produced by our wants, and government by our wickedness; the former promotes our happiness positively by uniting our affections, the latter negatively by restraining our vices."[1] This propaganda was published in a pamphlet that called for American independence from Britain. Paine referred to a divine ordinance and compared the geographical location of America and Britain to advocate for self-determination through revolution. The idea was to develop a system that would determine the extent to which the government asserts its authority over people to provide the necessary benefits for

1. Paine, *Common Sense*, 65.

society without becoming too intrusive, as was the case in Britain during Paine's time. It is impossible to control any synthetically designed social system that promotes the interests of the population while suppressing the system's natural authoritarian tendencies.

During the time of America's developmental phase, most European countries were monarchies, meaning their form of government relied on some form of centralized planning. After the US government was established and reforms took place in developed countries such as France, many countries held to a centrally planned society. This system of government continued to evolve into the modern age. Benito Mussolini firmly believed that the more complicated societies became, the more restricted the individual must be. According to Austrian economist F. A. Hayek, Mussolini received his ideology about restrictions on individual freedom from Marxist ideas. The ideology follows: To obtain a utopia for a society in the modernized era, a government must prevent monopolies from dominating industries. Thus, centralized planning is initiated, and industry is taken out of the private sector and controlled exclusively by the government.[2]

The development and collapse of the Soviet Union strongly oppose any long-term beneficial claims to centralized planning in society. The group responsible for the revolutions in Russia was the *intelligentsia*; they were credited with spreading revolutionary tendencies. Rebellions occur in every society, but how or if they are resolved depends on the population's trust in the functionality of the system versus how well professional agitators present their alternative

2. Hayek, *Road to Serfdom*, 91, 94.

system to citizens. During Russia's revolutionary phase, certain intellectual leaders in Russia viewed themselves as the ancient Greek and Roman philosophers whose job was to intervene in the lives of citizens. While ordinary citizens pursued a living, the intellectuals were the only ones with the knowledge to engineer the sciences of human affairs. They dismissed theories in classical economics and political theory, viewing them as irrelevant due to being formed as a result of sound principles—reason, logic, combined with trial and error. They swayed public opinion and many of these leaders evolved into an *intelligentsia* as they became politicians free to pursue their private ambitions in the guise of working for the common good. This intellectual ideology was based on materialism regarding humans not as unique individuals with immortal souls but as exclusively physical entities produced by their environment. This justifies their desire to engineer "a new breed of perfectly virtuous creatures"[3] through the restructuring of society.

Once in power, the intellectuals murdered the Romanovs, thereby ending monarchical rule in Russia. However, the centrally planned Soviet government proved to be no more beneficial for the Russian people; one autocracy had replaced another. The Soviet regime lasted most of the twentieth century. Proxy wars were fought abroad to influence various regions with communist ideology. The Afghan–Soviet War created additional disillusionment in the communist system that spread throughout their society, contributing to the collapse of the Soviet Empire.[4] Only

3. Pipes, *Concise History*, 21, 31.
4. Steele, *Philosophy of War*, 29.

one of the two superpowers that emerged from World War
II has survived. The United States embraced a semblance of
free markets, democracy, and limited government. However, a restricted government and economic freedom was an
illusion, a lost cause for Austrian economists, and a quasi-
approach by global Keynesians. The Keynesians needed a
large centralized government because it was essential for
their existence.

It's becoming more challenging to correctly deduce
meaning from a past that continues to be manipulated to
support reigning ideological trends. Ideally, the government's role should be extremely limited. Unfortunately, this
is an idea that cannot be brought to fruition because the
very nature of any political system, designated to rule or
guide humanity, has an unlimited quest for power. It also
expects total obedience from its subjects. It's absurd or extremely naïve to believe a political system can be contained
(or limited) via a self-produced document from the system
dictating the rules for governors. If the self-prescribed rules
get in the way of absolute authority, the rules are ignored,
or the judiciary will interpret/amend the document for
the benefit of the system. The dichotomy between manu-
factured crises and artificial social movements carried out
via professional agitators is evidence of a failing system.
The question is, how far will the ruling class go to save the
failing system? The populace has already proven their obedience, both symbolically and in action, priming the necessary conditions for more tyrannical policy to be enforced
by their beloved government.[5] Nevertheless, it's doubtful
that at any point society will relinquish its misconceptions

5. See He and Laurent, "World Is Masking Up"; and Dunford, "Coronavirus."

of government (even when taking the form of a republic), believing that it somehow can grant humanity the best possible life, and without it, there can be no civilization. The latter belief, i.e., a civilized society depends on government, is ironic considering global or large-scale war would be impossible without organized societies. Like all governments that adhere to the centralized-planned system, the United States cannot elude the hell that follows.

Most scholars in the academy are not capable of freeing their institutionalized minds. By the time these scholars finish graduate school, they are fully indoctrinated, and most aspire to work for the institutions that helped to form their worldview. Scholars who are not affiliated with the academy are confronted with a multifaceted campaign of misinformation when trying to understand the human condition. Once the fragmented pieces of the past are collected, there is the challenge of deciphering biased depictions of events recorded in the historiography by the victors.

To add to this complexity, there is the diversity, equality, and inclusion (DEI) movement that is dedicated to discrediting European and Western accomplishments by insisting they were driven by racism, imperialism, and bigotry. They argue that developing tribes and nations would have been more advanced, even surpassing the West, had they not been enslaved by these aggressors. The protected classes, mostly made up of the proletariat, are ignorant of these campaigns. Instead, they believe the prevailing narrative, i.e., they have been victimized. Further, any opposing views are nothing more than a conspiracy intended to be a distraction that will prevent DEI policy from advancing. By promoting DEI ideology, institutions have created resentment among the protected classes toward WASP.

The only group that has benefited from this calamity is those in the upper echelons of society, that is, oligarchies or lifelong politicians. This group is not impacted by the social disarray and economic chaos. They are the overseers of the system and control society indirectly via media and institutions. Centralized governments fund special programs for protected classes by taxing the bourgeoisie. The bourgeoisie are no more enlightened than the proletariat when it comes to control mechanisms of centralized planned societies because, for generations, they have been educated by state-affiliated institutions. Religious universities are not exempt from spreading this ideology because they receive government funding. Most religious institutions have no qualms about promoting DEI programs. Media outlets are applicable in the process; essentially, they are a mouthpiece for the centralized system. Media outlets popularize DEI ideology, which prompts religious leaders to adjust their message accordingly, hoping to appease their members. Most religious institutions are indistinguishable from secular institutions; they promote the same political policies, i.e., LGBTQ+, the transgender movement, and women's reproductive rights (abortion). A few decades ago, rather than embrace these ideologies, religious institutions would make persuasive attempts at ministering to those who held such views. Currently, some laws prevent religious organizations from intervening in the lives of those mentioned above.[6]

6. In the United States, California state law prohibits licensed professionals from offering rehabilitation programs for homosexuals under the age of eighteen years old. See Victor, "Regulating Sexual Orientation."

2

The Keynesian Saga

The complex monetary system is designed to manipulate and control economies via centralized planning. The Keynesian model is promoted heavily in academic institutions. Economists rely on Vector Autoregression (VAR) models to forecast macroeconomic time series that may infer the effects of structural shocks and estimate unobservable cyclical components of macroeconomic aggregates. A VAR model consists of a system of equations that represents the relationships between multiple variables. For example, variables such as unemployment, interest, and inflation rates may be incorporated into a VAR model. Theories claim to improve model misspecification, thereby avoiding inaccuracies.[1] These models are interesting, but the substrate on which any economic framework rests should take priority. In the absence of classical economic theory, a model, regardless of complexity, cannot correspond to economic realities or provide

1. Loria et al, "Economic Theories."

real-world solutions. The Keynesian econometric framework, which nearly all models are based on, possesses fallacious twentieth-century concepts regarding centralized planning and a demand-driven economy.

The well-known regression techniques associated with the Gibbs sampler or Bayesian statistics, integrated and exploited in new VAR models, are not in question. These statistical models are useful, but the underlying assumptions (*ex ante*) should be based on classical economic theory before the theoretical structure (*ex post*) can be expected to yield real solutions. As Jean-Baptiste Say stated, "The study of statistics may gratify curiosity, but it can never be productive of advantage when it does not indicate the origin and consequences of the facts it has collected; and by indicating their origin and consequences, it at once becomes the science of political economy."[2] Economic theory cannot be based solely on statistical data because human affairs and economies are too complex. Statistical models cannot provide cause and effect without incorporating what Say understood as political economy. He articulates how Adam Smith used a combination of statistics and political economy to develop his theory. However, the term statistics was not defined precisely as it is now. Statistics in Say's time referenced the numerical data collected and did not include probability as our contemporary models do. Today, talented statisticians can manipulate data to satisfy the politically influenced economic system.

It's important to notice how solutions are defined, specifically when integrating statistical models with the Keynesian apparatus. Solutions are defined by a workable

2. Say, *Treatise on Political Economy*, 19.

model, not by actually solving the problem within the physical framework. Models containing GDP variables further exacerbate forecast reliability.[3] This is especially true when projections are made based on GDP gaps. Determining potential GDP is controversial, as there is a lack of consensus among economists as to how it should be measured. Generally, potential output is based on full employment. The forecast can be enigmatic, e.g., in 2020, during the height of COVID-19 lockdowns, the Federal Reserve Bank of St. Louis had projected the fourth-quarter potential GDP to be $19.41 trillion. However, the actual GDP was $21.48 trillion.[4] The positive GDP gap is puzzling, considering many sectors of the US economy had cut or ceased production, and many employees were at home.

Keynesian economic theory is the primary influence on any model; the VAR is no exception. The VAR model forecast is based on prior results (e.g., VARIABLEt-1). The formulas connected with the data may produce results satisfactory to a statistician's expectations. The question is, how useful are these workable models on the macro side? Some of the latest research suggests significant improvements have been made in forecasting by noting the marginal possibility of conjugate priors commonly used and embedding the VAR into a Gibbs sampler to allow for multiple measurements from each economic variable.[5]

The microeconomic side or managerial side in manufacturing may benefit more from VAR models, but lean production methods have ensured that surpluses will be

3. See appendix for an example of a VAR model in R.
4. Majaski, "Output Gap."
5. See Loria et al., "Economic Theories."

essentially nonexistent. The nonexistent surplus has created a plethora of issues, beginning with the lockdowns in 2020. These critiques are parallel to what Steven Kates noticed, revealing the false dichotomy between a downturn in the economy and demand.[6] The equations, data, and model may be sound and workable, but the false assumptions based on faulty economic theory often fail to return real-world solutions.

KEYNESIAN REVOLUTION

All modern economists who specialize in the study of macroeconomics have been inundated with Keynesian thought. Keynesian models are structured around the belief that variations in aggregate demand are the basis for explaining variations in output and employment. Aggregate demand is distinct from effective demand (a term that dates back to the eighteenth century), which is concerned with what must occur when an individual decides to purchase products. Aggregate demand was brought into economic discourse in 1936 by John Maynard Keynes. This definition included all individual demands within an economy.[7]

Keynes focused on monetary aggregates, i.e., saving and investing were thought of in money terms. Value is not considered, or what some classical economists refer to as the real side of the economy—production. Economic growth in terms of production is replaced by this new focus on the monetary. National saving was compared with individual saving. Savings on an individual level were viewed as

6 Kates, "Keynesian Concepts," 6.

7. Kates, "Keynesian Concepts," 4.

detrimental to the economy, and those who spent all their income were viewed as providing stimulus to the economy. Therefore, spending was preferred over savers who hoarded income, which led to an economic recession. Keynes's theory holds that centralized planning by governments could control a nation's spending, thereby stimulating the economy via spending. The Keynesian theory insists that economic downturns occur because of unplanned hoarding by individuals or banks. The shrinkage in aggregate demand will influence production, i.e., it will encourage reductions in aggregate supply. Only government spending can create the necessary conditions for returning to equilibrium between aggregate demand and supply.

The General Theory of Keynes is prevalent in contemporary macroeconomic practice, e.g., the current trend combines government spending with monetary policy via the Federal Reserve, attempting to lower wages and increase unemployment. This combination is believed to address two problems: recession and inflation. The spending will return demand levels and pull the nation from a possible recession, and the Fed's policy will provide an avenue for wage reduction and higher unemployment, which will reduce inflation. Many have noticed that reducing wages and raising unemployment seem antithetical to creating conditions for a better economy.

JEAN-BAPTISTE SAY'S TREATISE

Keynes's theory has had serious problems from its inception. It is fallacious to think of national savings in such terms (monetary). Nations do not save by hoarding money in financial institutions as individuals do. A nation's savings consists of raw materials and productive assets that can be used to transform inputs into a final output for future returns. The nation's potential to produce a product constitutes its savings; it has little to do with the monetary. The nation's production capacity is the real side of the economy understood by classical economists.

Jean-Baptiste Say, near the turn of the nineteenth century (c. 1803), composed a treatise that centered on a concept, i.e., all economic activity began on the supply side. This became known as Say's Law of Markets, and it was universally accepted until 1936.[8] It was not part of the new science of economics taught by classical economists of the time, but, as Ludwig von Mises elaborated, it was "a preliminary—the exposure and removal of garbled and untenable ideas which dimmed people's minds and were a serious obstacle to a reasonable analysis of conditions."[9] Before Adam Smith's and Say's theories, there were two reasons given for a business failure: the scarcity of money and overproduction. In a passage from his *Wealth of Nations*, Smith exposed the fallacy regarding money scarcity. For this section, however, we are concerned with Say's treatise and what proved to be a myth regarding overproduction and business failure.

There can never be an absolute overproduction of economic goods. There will always be unsatisfied needs that a larger supply of certain economic goods can satisfy. There may, of course, be relative overproduction. This stems from an error in management where a certain good

8. Kates, "Keynesian Concepts" 6.
9. Mises, "Keynes and Say's Law," 1.

underperforms compared to its related counterpart. The management has misread market conditions and produced too much of one good and likely too little of another. In Mises's analysis of Say's Law, he provided the example of shirts and shoes. If consumers are purchasing a larger quantity of shoes and a smaller quantity of shirts, this is not an indication of overproduction of all commodities.[10] It is rather an error in management; they have failed to understand the needs or desires of their customers, i.e., they have failed to anticipate the conditions of the market. A classical economist would never interpret such a scenario as a general depression, nor would they consider it applicable to aggregate demand. The situation is improved by reversing the ratio of production between commodities. Here is where an argument can be made for VAR models. In manufacturing scenarios, where forecasts are based on priors, these models reveal trends that can assist managers with understanding future market conditions for correct production ratios. Again, the goal here is not to discourage the use of such models on a microscale. Problems emerge when models are used in conjunction with Keynesian theory, or when they are used to justify overall production cuts.

Say and Smith dispelled the myth that periods of bad business were caused by scarcity of money and absolute overproduction. Many classical economists have demonstrated that recurring depressions of trade were caused by repeated attempts to stimulate the economy via government spending and credit expansion. They did, however, concede that credit expansion would create an initial boom in business, but it would inevitably be followed by a bust.

10. Mises, "Keynes and Say's Law," 3.

Their theories held until the so-called Keynesian revolution took precedence (some economists argue it wasn't a revolution). True statesmen could see value in classical economic theory for the prosperity of their nation, but the career politician found no use for it. Or, as Mises eloquently stated, "It could not influence demagogues who care for nothing but success in the impending election campaign and are not in the least troubled about what will happen the day after tomorrow."[11] These politicians build their wealth from wars at the expense of the proletariat and perpetuate their power via centralized planning. Free markets have no place in their artificial economy constructed of fiat money and empty promises of prosperity through spending.

Moreover, the aggregate demand fallacy and its solution, i.e., government spending, were policies already adopted by politicians before Keynes's book, *General Theory*, was published. According to some economists, Keynes wrote it as an apology for the policies already in place by governments. Keynes's work provided the semblance of a scientific allure that could be touted before their constituents. It also provided credence for the mathematical economist who treasured the workable model over a reality-based solution.

THE SAGA CONTINUES

In consideration of the classical economic view, it may be beneficial to note the economic calamity that has begun to unfold since 2020. The Keynesian theory is well integrated into the universities that have produced managers who

11. Mises, "Keynes and Say's Law," 7.

acquire positions at major manufacturing facilities in the United States. Upper management seems to prefer mid-managers who boast of their credentials, proudly displaying their black belt certification in Six Sigma. The JIT lean production methodology is compatible with the aggregate demand theory. This philosophy emerged from Japan after WWII and found its way to the United States in the 1970s. The focus is not simply on looking for ways to improve cost by creating more efficient production systems. A portion of the process entails cutting storage costs by eliminating surplus. Auto manufacturing adheres to these JIT practices as they do not store large surpluses of parts. The parts they need to complete the production process arrive just in time and are immediately incorporated into the assembly.

VAR models can certainly improve forecasts, but they should be understood through the lens of relative supply and effective demand. This is especially true for manufacturing when it comes to production ratios. During the 2020 lockdowns, products were redirected to areas that could sustain relative supply and effective demand. The market conditions were changing, artificially via government intrusion, but changing nonetheless. Auto manufacturing, for a time, ceased and semiconductors that were being produced for new vehicles were repurposed and made readily available for electronic devices. Their ability to improvise is noteworthy, but they were short-sighted regarding another sector: they should have continued producing for auto manufacturers as well. This would have resulted in relative overproduction but it would soon be alleviated once the government took its hand off the scale.

If nothing else becomes of the 2020 totalitarian exercise, it should at least solidify that the nation's production apparatus is the real side of the economy, i.e., supply drives economies, and aggregate demand is a fallacy. Moreover, government spending causes significant inflation and its interference in production cripples the supply chain. Although, if there is a substantial surplus, many businesses can weather economic crises far better. The theoretical structure that Jean-Baptiste Say and Adam Smith helped develop could have spared us from the disastrous, failed Keynesian-based economy, but they are viewed by the ruling class as antiquated and antithetical to government. In truth, governments will not likely retire Keynesian economic theory, as too much is at risk for the politician. Relinquishing control of the economy where government officials have the power to essentially choose winners and losers via illusionary mechanisms of a failed theory, as opposed to allowing a truly free market to persist, is incomprehensible for the politician.

3

Historical Interpretation

G etting massive numbers of people to accept new concepts usually requires a systematic approach. A system must be engineered and thoroughly embedded into every aspect of social life. It must start early and be continuous throughout a person's lifespan. All institutions, religious and academic, have a role in this system. How history is recorded is perhaps the key to the functionality of this system. Herodotus was an ancient Greek historian from the fifth century BCE.[1] He sought to use verifiable sources to extract information from the past, developing the model that historians continue to follow today. The issue with constructing a narrative of what occurred in the past is that it cannot be exactly replicated. Generally, this is because a considerable amount of information is missing, lost, or destroyed. Historians construct fragments of the past and consider society and cultural influence when developing a narrative. They fill in gaps based on historical

1. Gilderhus, *History and Historians*, 5.

evidence and produce an interpretation of the past. However, remnants from the past can be manipulated when a skilled rhetorician has an agenda. The historians tell us their interpretation of the past based on surviving fragments used to construct a narrative of what they believe happened. Historical interpretation will always depend on the interpreter's worldview.

Historiography refers to the history of historical writing in broad terms. In a narrower sense, it refers to the specific area in history that will be investigated. Every topic has its history, and we should avoid judging historical events through a contemporary lens. Future generations may develop ways to understand the world that cannot be fathomed in the current age; cultural practices, traditions, and social norms of this era will seem backward to future generations studying it.

Attempting to analyze historical events using existing fragments and prevailing institutionalized ideologies, as mentioned in the introduction of this composition, seems counterproductive and even contradictory. For instance, any collection from the fragmented record used to form a narrative will be shaped by the historian's biased worldview. In other cases, the narrative will be adjusted to accommodate the demands of those who have acquired the historian's services. It is equivalent to someone who claims statements are invalid and then refers back to them to make their point. This problem is noticeable in the *Discourses of Epictetus* when he remarked, "Nothing is universally true" or "If any truth is universal, it is false."[2] However, this argument seeks to show how difficult and problematic it can be

2. Dobbin, *Epictetus*, 128.

to extract or accept prevailing truths derived from history; it does not claim truth is unattainable. From an adjunct's perspective, i.e., someone who assists with teaching history at a university, these problems are apparent. The institution has a specified way the information is to be presented to students by the professor. History professors are more than willing to ignore all their training and present a one-sided view of the past. These biased views are driven by political ideologies promoted by the institutionalized system. Not all of the participants are aware of the problem. Some of the less intellectually equipped professors prove to be useful in spreading this ideology, especially in lower-tiered universities. These professors are true believers, refusing to entertain any opposition to their one-sided view. Generally, they are not allowed to teach at prestigious institutions; they can be found teaching at large religious universities and sometimes two-year state colleges.

Government institutions control academia via federal funds. In the spring of 2024, many university students began to protest on campuses across the United States. This was a reaction to the news coming out of the Middle East.[3] The International Criminal Court and the International Court of Justice both called for investigations into alleged genocide committed by the Israel Defense Forces in Gaza.[4] In response to these protests, US lawmakers introduced the Antisemitism Awareness Act. This law mandates that the US Department of Education adopt the definition of antisemitism used by the International Holocaust Remembrance Alliance. The definition of antisemitism is broad.

---

3. International Criminal Court, "State of Palestine."
4. International Court of Justice, *Application*.

Essentially, any negative perception of Jews that is expressed may be counted as antisemitism, e.g., believing that passages in the New Testament are correct regarding the Jews and how they gave Jesus over to the Romans to be crucified would count as violating the act. Some religious schools could jeopardize their federal funding should they choose to uphold their doctrinal beliefs regarding the inspiration and reliability of their religious texts. The institutionalized media, fulfilling their role, promise viewers this will not be a problem, i.e., the law will not be as tyrannical as it sounds. Whether the bill passes or not, the relevant point for mentioning this is that it shows the interconnections of the institutionalized system and how it deals with perceived threats. When this work was being composed, the bill was still making its way through legislation. It passed in the House and is now awaiting consideration in the Senate.[5]

There is a classical notion derived from the Greeks that no one ever teaches anyone anything; for instance, Socrates argued that philosophy is self-taught. Aside from learning basic language structure, each individual will interpret written or oral information based on their prior knowledge. The individual receiving the message will interpret it according to the speaker's or writer's intent, or they may interpret it incorrectly based on their preconceived notions. Thus, disagreements arise from those who do not occupy the same reality. Those who share a common culture and moral values will comprehend each other much more accurately and will seldom have disagreements.

The preferred method to bring everyone into the same reality is indoctrination. Social engineers will assign a high

5. See the Antisemitism Awareness Act of 2025.

value to what they believe is essential to the functionality of a system. Once these essential properties are defined, everyone in the system must be converted, seduced, or indoctrinated to accept the value of these properties. A system that has established institutions will ensure the continuation of the process. Most inhabitants of the system will surrender their judgment to these institutions because they promise to relieve the inhabitants of their uncertainties and ignorance via welfare and public education.[6] The process of indoctrination will be less effective for certain individuals. This is because they prefer seduction over indoctrination, i.e., they are willing to accept the properties provided a logical reason can be offered. The simplest example is language, i.e., using the phrase women's reproductive rights rather than abortion may persuade the skeptic to accept the essential properties of the system.

SPECULATIVE AND ANALYTICAL HISTORY

Speculative philosophy of history attempts to construct an all-encompassing history—a universal history that accounts for the rise and decline of empires, states, and cultures. Modern historians have substituted the practice of connecting major events to the unfolding of history on a grand scale for narrowly focused specialist studies. "History proper," as noted by scholar M. C. Lemon, has mostly been phased out and replaced with controversial contemporary social studies, encompassing a range of ideological

---

6. Derived from the analysis on perspectivism and absolutism in Calhoun, *Theodicy*, 29–36.

concerns.[7] Speculative philosophy of history is concerned with analyzing the content of history as a whole to extract a meaningful account of the past. It takes into account the various mentalities over the ages and contemplates what mechanism controls the course of human history, i.e., Does Fate or Providence have a role? The emergence of modern science and social studies, at least in the contemporary sense, has discounted this philosophical approach to history.[8] Analytic philosophy of history critically examines the process historians apply to their discipline. They critique the historian's methods for obtaining information related to the past and question whether or not the narrative results in historical knowledge. Philosophy of history is concerned with both of these branches, speculative and analytic. The speculative treats history as a large unfolding of human affairs in the past. Thereby, it searches for meaningful connections by approaching history as an "object." Analytic philosophy of history treats history as an academic discipline by critiquing the speculative approach. In other words, the analytic branch studies history "for its own sake," collecting facts and reporting events; it is not concerned with assigning meaning to the past.[9]

Whatever argument can be made regarding approaches to studying history, there exist two primary obstacles that impact both the speculative and the analytical. These obstacles are the so-called collection of facts and the interpretation of these facts. After reviewing Herodotus's *The Histories*, the reader will discover some outrageous

7. Lemon, *Philosophy of History*, 1–2.

8. Lemon, *Philosophy of History*, 8–9.

9. Steele, *Philosophy of Qohelet*, 6.

accounts. Herodotus shares the same view as most ancients did during this era, i.e., he believed that deities often intervened in human affairs. He wrote about Apollo at Delphi, a god who communicated through a priestess. This was one of the most important oracles the Greeks sought advice from before taking any important action. Herodotus's historical narratives consisted of stories from eyewitness accounts of superhuman heroes helping them. While he does nothing to discredit these stories, he attempts to distance himself from them with statements such as "It is said." He also invented speeches of prominent historical figures, putting words in their mouths to provide structure and an interesting narrative that his readers could follow. For these reasons, many contemporary historians are critical of Herodotus, even branding him "the father of lies," rather than "the father of history."

Modern scholars who charge Herodotus with distorted and inaccurate accounts of history suffer from many of the same problems. The conflict that began in 2014 between Ukraine and Russia is a good example. The West has decided to build a narrative that portrays Russian President Vladimir Putin as a tyrant who has decided to embark on an unprovoked conquest of his neighboring countries. In 2014, Germany and France brokered a deal with Russia titled the Minsk Agreements. The protocols were initiated because of the dispute between Ukraine and Russia over the territory of Crimea. Crimea decided to join Russia in 2014 following a Western-backed coup in Kyiv. The coup in Kyiv resulted in Volodymyr Zelensky becoming the president of Ukraine. At the direction of Washington, Zelensky began to advocate for NATO membership in addition to promoting his "peace formula," which called for Russia to surrender all territories claimed by Kyiv and pay reparations. Putin made it clear that Ukraine's joining NATO was a red line for Russia. Russia did not want NATO missiles placed on its borders. It was later discovered that signing the Minsk Agreements was a delay tactic by the West to allow Ukraine to build up its military and prepare for a conflict with Russia.[10] Nevertheless, propaganda continues to be touted by the media, i.e., Russia is the aggressor and will not stop at the Polish border. Cliché parallels from World War II are made by political commentators, certain Democrat and Republican senators, and members of the US Congress who will likely profit from the conflict. Fortunes have been made at the expense of Ukrainian and Russian lives. Billions of US dollars in support of Ukraine are split between the Zelensky regime and the industrial war complex in the United States. It is all too predictable how historians will record the Russian-Ukrainian conflict.

The point here was to demonstrate examples of control the system uses. Legislation was introduced to protect a country accused of genocide. The Israeli lobbyists are a source of income to many US lawmakers. Federal aid provided to Israel from the United States makes its way back to members of Congress. The media are consistently disingenuous regarding Eastern Europe and the conflict between Russia and Ukraine. The billions allocated to Ukraine will enrich the US industrial war complex and its associates. The official recorded history, however, will likely reflect a different narrative. It will likely portray Israel as defending itself from what they have referred to as a Holocaust initiated by

10. See the collection of sources at RT, "Russia–Ukraine Conflict."

Hamas on October 7, 2023.[11] Vladimir Putin will likely be compared to Hitler, who is determined to rule all of Europe.[12] The educational system will prompt its professors to present this narrative to students as official historiography.

The Russians have insisted on many occasions that Ukraine's becoming a member of NATO was unacceptable. What strategic threat would it be to Western nations for Ukraine to remain a neutral state, and why does the United States need to support a nuclear-armed country in the Middle East? There isn't any threat, and Israel would be more cautious toward its neighbors without US support! Perhaps we need to reconsider the Monroe Doctrine of 1823. This doctrine was composed by John Quincy Adams and was delivered to Congress by President James Monroe. The doctrine warned European nations that the United States would not tolerate colonization or puppet monarchies in the Western Hemisphere. The US leaders were concerned with the islands in and around the Caribbean (Cuba was in danger of annexation by European powers at the time). The United States also declared that it would not interfere with European interests in Europe.[13] Essentially, the Americans were saying, stay out of our area of strategic influence, and we will stay out of yours. Nevertheless, the United States currently has roughly eight hundred bases in more than seventy countries; so much for the Monroe Doctrine.[14]

11. Wermenbol, "Post-October 7 Specter."

12. Blake, "Putin."

13. Compston and Seidman, *Our Documents*, 66–67.

14. Vine, "Where in the World."

4

Aristocracy

A ristotle's works have shaped Western thought for
nearly two thousand years. This section will provide
a simple overview of Aristotle's ideal government. In his
Politics, Aristotle systematically analyzes different forms of
government, distinguishing between correct and deviant
constitutions. Among the correct constitutions—kingship,
aristocracy, and polity—aristocracy holds a central place as
rule by the virtuous few for the common good. In Book
II, Aristotle critiques existing regimes, including Sparta
and Carthage, while outlining the characteristics of an
ideal aristocracy. His discussion of Carthage is particularly
instructive, as he regards it as a well-ordered constitution
that blends aristocratic and democratic elements.

Aristotle praises certain aspects of Sparta's mixed
constitution, while he criticizes its emphasis on military
virtue at the expense of other goods. He also notes their
unwillingness to protect the virtue of citizenship—they
were known to extend citizenship to strangers. His analysis

of Carthage, however, is more favorable, as he considers it a well-functioning aristocracy with democratic features. For example, he approves of Carthage's practice of selecting officials not only based on birth but also merit, which aligns with aristocratic principles. He does, however, criticize Carthage for excessively valuing wealth, as many offices required significant financial resources, leading to a drift toward oligarchy. Despite this flaw, Carthage's mixed constitution—combining aristocratic leadership with popular consent—ensured stability and prevented tyranny.[1]

NOBLE ARISTOCRACY

Aristotle defines aristocracy as the best government, where political power is vested in those who excel in virtue and are capable of ruling for the sake of the whole community. The oligarchy is ruled by the wealthy for their own benefit. The kingship is unlimited in its power and does not consult the people (Carthage had two annually elected magistrates similar to Spartan kings, but their power was limited). The aristocracy, however, is a just constitution because the ruling class is morally and intellectually superior. They are motivated to govern in the best interests of their citizens. Aristotle's ideal aristocracy differs from both Spartan militarism and Carthaginian plutocratic tendencies. He argues that the best constitution blends democratic and oligarchic elements while being guided by virtue. According to Aristotle, true aristocracy requires the following:

---

1. McKeon, *Basic Works of Aristotle*, 1165–73.

- Moral and intellectual excellence. Rulers must possess practical wisdom and justice to govern for the common good.

- Stable hierarchies. While birth plays a role, virtue must remain the primary criterion for office.

- Balanced institutions. A mixed constitution, like Carthage's but without its oligarchic leanings, ensures no single group dominates.

Aristotle concluded that a noble aristocracy emphasizes rule by the virtuous few, but he recognized the practical challenges of maintaining such a system. His analysis of Carthage in Book II demonstrates how a well-ordered aristocracy can incorporate popular participation while avoiding corruption. However, he insists that true aristocracy must prioritize virtue over wealth or birth, ensuring that governance serves the common good rather than private interests.

UNVIRTUOUS ARISTOCRACY

The French Revolution (1789–1799) is one of the most transformative events in modern history, marking the collapse of the Old Regime and the rise of democratic republicanism. Scholarly interpretations of the revolution have evolved significantly, with debates focusing on its causes, key phases, and long-term consequences. The causes of the revolution range from a financial crisis to a degenerate ruling class.[2] The monarchy's fiscal collapse was exacerbated by costly wars, including the American Revolution.

2. Alpaugh, "Self-Defining Bourgeoisie," 669–99.

Moreover, inefficient taxation forced Louis XVI to convene the Estates-General. The rigid three-estate system (clergy, nobility, commoners) bred resentment, particularly among the rising bourgeoisie.[3] Philosophers like Rousseau (The Social Contract) and Voltaire critiqued absolutism, promoting ideas of popular sovereignty. Perhaps the primary reason for the revolution was that the aristocracy had lost its honor and virtue. The population began to see the ruling class as morally unfit to rule.

1789 ON A GLOBAL SCALE

The geopolitical events unfolding over the last few years have created extreme resentment for the ruling class. Mass immigration, proxy wars, genocide, and the Epstein fiasco have both the proletariat and the bourgeoisie concerned. They have lost faith in the institutions and the leaders' abilities to rule. The economy has been decimated, not just by the flood of illegal immigration, but by legal immigration as well. In the United States, Trump provided amnesty for the illegal immigrants he campaigned on deporting. If they worked at one of his hotels, they were given immunity from deportation (or in certain areas of the service sector, farms, etc.).[4] H-1B, H-1B1, and E-3 visas have made it a significant challenge for US citizens seeking employment. Amazon, Apple, NVIDIA, Goldman Sachs, and Microsoft have been among the worst offenders in laying off employees, only to apply for these foreign visas. The common trend among these companies is to blame advances in artificial

3. Alpaugh, "Self-Defining Bourgeoisie," 697–98.
4. Axelrod, "MAGA on 'Amnesty Watch.'"

intelligence for their decision to lay off workers. The real motivation is that companies can acquire foreign workers at a much lower cost through the visas mentioned above. Initially, these foreign workers were, in theory, intended to fill "high-skill" roles, but the data tell a different story. According to reports from The Hill, 82 percent of Microsoft's H-1B applications for 2025 have been for positions the department classifies as Level I or II—entry or mid-level roles paid at or below the 34th wage percentile.[5]

The proxy war in Ukraine may be about to come to an end as the Russians continue to make strategic gains and the Ukrainian lines begin to collapse. Trump successfully secured a meeting with Putin in mid-August 2025. The diplomatic process appeared last-minute and rushed, suggesting the military situation in Ukraine could be much worse than reported by Western media.[6] The genocide in Gaza is slowly capturing the attention of the public via independent journalists, which has pressured some leaders to take notice,[7] although it could be nothing more than virtue signaling to appease their constituents. If the proxy war ends in Ukraine, it will have a devastating impact on the psyche of the European leaders who believe Russia is the last stronghold to completing the global agenda. Russia still promotes traditional values and is unwilling to abide by the unipolar progressive ideologies of the West. The United States, however, will turn its attention back to the Middle East. Perhaps they'll decide Iran needs to be

---

5. Takala, "H-1Bs are Wreaking Havoc."

6. Kashin, "Behind the Illusion."

7. Stanley-Smith, "19 EU Countries Condemn."

destroyed because new intelligence suggests Iran continues to pursue a nuclear weapons program.

The Epstein fiasco may be the United States's Marie Antoinette prompt. Trump's base has lost faith in him because the issue he campaigned on is now a hoax, according to him. He was clearly disturbed by questions regarding Epstein and announced he didn't want anyone's support who continued to push for answers on the Epstein files. The Epstein issue extends beyond the United States, as world leaders and high-profile individuals were involved or associated with Epstein's sex-trafficking network. Dozens of names associated with Epstein were mentioned in a release of court documents in 2024. Among the names were Prince Andrew and former US presidents. Both the former US presidents and the British royal deny any knowledge of Epstein's crimes.[8] Rumors persist that Epstein was a Mossad agent and an FBI informant. The problem is that, regardless of its truth, the ruling class and elites have repeatedly lied and been exposed for engaging in unvirtuous acts, leading the public to be willing to entertain these allegations. Nevertheless, these allegations don't need to be true because there's enough evidence for the population to conclude the ruling class is unfit to rule. The question is what will they do?

8. Geoghegan and FitzGerald, "Epstein Files."

Conclusion

Postmodern rhetoric related to the new social construct of the twenty-first century advocates for a single approach to social issues by dramatizing the alternative. The hyperbole associated with this rhetoric demonizes all alternative views, typically by associating them with misanthropic intentions. This type of rhetoric is not exclusive to the postmodern era; it has been in circulation since antiquity. However, the equality-driven agenda integrated into nearly every institution has a devastating impact on individuals; it has produced an unintelligent, docile subject. This movement is well organized and extends into society's social fabric to include educational, political, and religious institutions.

The shifting social patterns brought about by DEI ideology, through mass immigration and supported by nearly every institution, will be a topic of debate for social scientists and historians for many years to come. However, certain Eastern European countries have renewed their attitudes toward conservative principles. Hungary, Russia, and others appear to be embracing the values that the West was once known to safeguard. Perhaps the solution lies in the bourgeoisie uniting with the proletariat, urging them toward a genuine awakening, one that contrasts with the totalitarian system imposed by the intelligentsia at the expense of the working class in the early twentieth century or the destructive DEI ideology of this century—an Aristotelian approach modified to extend into society in the form of a noble aristocracy. It would be nationalistic in that small communities would consist of residents who hold the same values and cultural traits. This would prevent the victimization of individuals who previously subscribed to the failed political systems established by elites and their empty promises of a future utopia in the form of monarchy, oligarchy, or large-scale democracies. These unorganized, loosely structured, localized communities, where individuality is valued and mobs are held in contempt, would be an abomination to contemporary political and religious thought. This is because, primarily, it wouldn't require people to exchange their sovereignty and freedoms for an illusory existence of peace, prosperity, and security. It would require large-scale, homogeneous participation (globally) to dismantle or reject institutions to a manageable point, where, if they existed at all, they would be forced to succumb to the will of the population (the inverse of the current system).

Is it a fool's errand? Perhaps, but there's a strange enigma regarding the cognition of the enslaved that will not allow them to, at some point, demand that the ruling elites stop manufacturing social and economic problems, thereby allowing them to live their own lives on their terms. It is certainly not an intellectual problem—too many people fully comprehend their situation. However, the stigma of resistance, coupled with deeply ingrained doctrines of democracy, via institutions, from birth to grave, generation after generation, has ensured that most will never act contrary to the system.

Appendix

Var_fred.R

joels

2025-07-26

```r
rm(list = ls())
# ================================================
# VAR MODEL WITH FRED API INTEGRATION - OPTIMIZED
# ================================================


# 1. INITIAL SETUP ----------------------------------------------------

# Set CRAN mirror and silent warnings
options(repos = c(CRAN = "https://cloud.r-project.org"),
        warn = -1,
        stringsAsFactors = FALSE)

# 2. PACKAGE MANAGEMENT ------------------------------------------------

# Install and load required packages
if (!require("pacman")) install.packages("pacman", quiet = TRUE)
```

Loading required package: pacman

```r
suppressPackageStartupMessages({
  pacman::p_load(
    fredr,         # FRED API interface
    vars,          # VAR modeling
    ggplot2,       # Visualization
    urca,          # Stationarity tests
    tidyverse,     # Data manipulation
    xts,           # Time series handling
    lubridate,     # Date operations
    knitr,         # Reporting
    tinytex        # For PDF output
  )

  # Install TinyTeX if missing (for PDF reports)
  if (!tinytex::is_tinytex()) tinytex::install_tinytex()
})

# 3. FRED API CONFIGURATION --------------------------------------------

# Set FRED API key
fredr_set_key("ef9099c31be32d2d176053093d5bca95")
```

1

Appendix

```
# 4. DATA ACQUISITION FUNCTION -----------------------------------------------

get_fred_data <- function() {
  # Define FRED series IDs with clear naming
  series_ids <- c(
    GDP = "GDPC1",        # Real GDP (Quarterly)
    CPI = "CPIAUCSL",     # Consumer Price Index (Monthly)
    UNRATE = "UNRATE"     # Unemployment Rate (Monthly)
  )

  # Set date range (8 years back from today)
  start_date <- Sys.Date() - lubridate::years(8)
  end_date <- Sys.Date()

  # Fetch all series with error handling
  fred_data <- purrr::imap_dfr(series_ids, ~ {
    tryCatch({
      fredr(
        series_id = .x,
        observation_start = start_date,
        observation_end = end_date,
        frequency = ifelse(.y == "GDP", "q", "m") # Quarterly for GDP
      ) %>%
        mutate(variable = .y) %>%
        select(date, variable, value)
    }, error = function(e) {
      message("Error fetching ", .y, ": ", e$message)
      return(NULL)
    })
  })

  # Process data: convert monthly to quarterly and merge
  gdp_data <- fred_data %>%
    filter(variable == "GDP") %>%
    select(date, GDP = value)

  monthly_data <- fred_data %>%
    filter(variable != "GDP") %>%
    pivot_wider(names_from = variable, values_from = value)

  # Convert monthly to quarterly by averaging
  quarterly_other <- monthly_data %>%
    mutate(qtr = as.Date(lubridate::floor_date(date, "quarter"))) %>%
    group_by(qtr) %>%
    summarize(
      CPI = mean(CPI, na.rm = TRUE),
      UNRATE = mean(UNRATE, na.rm = TRUE)
    ) %>%
    rename(date = qtr)

  # Combine all series with proper date alignment
  full_data <- full_join(gdp_data, quarterly_other, by = "date") %>%
    arrange(date) %>%
```

2

Appendix

```
    na.omit() # Remove incomplete observations

  return(full_data)
}

# 5. DATA PREPARATION ---------------------------------------------------

# Get the economic data
economic_data <- get_fred_data()

# Convert to time series object with proper dates
ts_data <- ts(
  economic_data[, -1], # Exclude date column
  start = c(lubridate::year(min(economic_data$date)),
            lubridate::quarter(min(economic_data$date))),
  frequency = 4
)

# 6. STATIONARITY CHECKING ---------------------------------------------

# Check stationarity for each series
stationarity_tests <- apply(ts_data, 2, function(x) {
  test <- urca::ur.df(x, type = "drift")
  list(
    test_stat = test@teststat[1],
    critical_value = test@cval[1, "5pct"],
    is_stationary = test@teststat[1] < test@cval[1, "5pct"]
  )
})

# Print stationarity results
cat("\nStationarity Test Results:\n")


##
## Stationarity Test Results:

print(stationarity_tests)


## $GDP
## $GDP$test_stat
## [1] -0.4262503
##
## $GDP$critical_value
## [1] -2.93
##
## $GDP$is_stationary
## [1] FALSE
##
##
## $CPI
## $CPI$test_stat
## [1] 0.285454
```

3

Appendix

```
##
## $CPI$critical_value
## [1] -2.93
##
## $CPI$is_stationary
## [1] FALSE
##
##
## $UNRATE
## $UNRATE$test_stat
## [1] -2.51841
##
## $UNRATE$critical_value
## [1] -2.93
##
## $UNRATE$is_stationary
## [1] FALSE
```

```
# Difference non-stationary series
ts_data_diff <- diff(ts_data)
ts_data_diff <- na.omit(ts_data_diff)
```

```
# 7. VAR MODEL ESTIMATION ---------------------------------------------
```

```
# Determine optimal lag length (max 4 lags for quarterly data)
lag_selection <- VARselect(ts_data_diff, lag.max = 4, type = "const")
optimal_lags <- lag_selection$selection["AIC(n)"]
cat("\nSelected lag order based on AIC:", optimal_lags, "\n")
```

```
##
## Selected lag order based on AIC: 1
```

```
# Estimate VAR model
var_model <- VAR(ts_data_diff, p = optimal_lags, type = "const")
```

```
# 8. MODEL DIAGNOSTICS ------------------------------------------------
```

```
# Model summary
cat("\nVAR Model Summary:\n")
```

```
##
## VAR Model Summary:
```

```
print(summary(var_model))
```

```
##
## VAR Estimation Results:
## =========================
## Endogenous variables: GDP, CPI, UNRATE
## Deterministic variables: const
## Sample size: 29
## Log Likelihood: -268.701
```

4

Appendix

```
## Roots of the characteristic polynomial:
## 0.7989 0.6692 0.6692
## Call:
## VAR(y = ts_data_diff, p = optimal_lags, type = "const")
##
##
## Estimation results for equation GDP:
## ======================================
## GDP = GDP.l1 + CPI.l1 + UNRATE.l1 + const
##
##           Estimate Std. Error t value Pr(>|t|)
## GDP.l1      1.2624     0.4235   2.981 0.006326 **
## CPI.l1     40.7761    42.5283   0.959 0.346842
## UNRATE.l1 387.1442    99.8405   3.878 0.000678 ***
## const    -141.2990   141.8747  -0.996 0.328821
## ---
## Signif. codes:  0 '***' 0.001 '**' 0.01 '*' 0.05 '.' 0.1 ' ' 1
##
##
## Residual standard error: 353.1 on 25 degrees of freedom
## Multiple R-Squared: 0.425,   Adjusted R-squared: 0.356
## F-statistic:  6.16 on 3 and 25 DF,  p-value: 0.002779
##
##
## Estimation results for equation CPI:
## ======================================
## CPI = GDP.l1 + CPI.l1 + UNRATE.l1 + const
##
##           Estimate Std. Error t value Pr(>|t|)
## GDP.l1    0.002088   0.001572   1.328  0.1962
## CPI.l1    0.887611   0.157876   5.622 7.52e-06 ***
## UNRATE.l1 0.843967   0.370634   2.277  0.0316 *
## const     0.037030   0.526676   0.070  0.9445
## ---
## Signif. codes:  0 '***' 0.001 '**' 0.01 '*' 0.05 '.' 0.1 ' ' 1
##
##
## Residual standard error: 1.311 on 25 degrees of freedom
## Multiple R-Squared: 0.5607,  Adjusted R-squared: 0.508
## F-statistic: 10.64 on 3 and 25 DF,  p-value: 0.0001082
##
##
## Estimation results for equation UNRATE:
## ======================================
## UNRATE = GDP.l1 + CPI.l1 + UNRATE.l1 + const
##
##           Estimate Std. Error t value Pr(>|t|)
## GDP.l1    -0.007173   0.001927  -3.722 0.001008 **
## CPI.l1    -0.280183   0.193513  -1.448 0.160078
## UNRATE.l1 -1.866376   0.454297  -4.108 0.000375 ***
## const      1.633336   0.645562   2.530 0.018076 *
## ---
## Signif. codes:  0 '***' 0.001 '**' 0.01 '*' 0.05 '.' 0.1 ' ' 1
##
```

5

Appendix

```
##
## Residual standard error: 1.607 on 25 degrees of freedom
## Multiple R-Squared: 0.4032,  Adjusted R-squared: 0.3316
## F-statistic:  5.63 on 3 and 25 DF,  p-value: 0.004328
##
##
##
## Covariance matrix of residuals:
##             GDP      CPI   UNRATE
## GDP    124671.2  299.018 -534.340
## CPI       299.0    1.718   -1.385
## UNRATE   -534.3   -1.385    2.581
##
## Correlation matrix of residuals:
##             GDP      CPI   UNRATE
## GDP      1.0000   0.6461 -0.9419
## CPI      0.6461   1.0000 -0.6577
## UNRATE  -0.9419  -0.6577  1.0000
```

```r
# Stability check (all roots should be < 1)
cat("\nModel Stability Check:\n")
```

```
##
## Model Stability Check:
```

```r
print(roots(var_model))
```

```
## [1] 0.7988643 0.6691512 0.6691512
```

```r
# Residual diagnostics
serial_test <- serial.test(var_model, lags.pt = 10, type = "PT.asymptotic")
normality_test <- normality.test(var_model)

cat("\nSerial Correlation Test:\n")
```

```
##
## Serial Correlation Test:
```

```r
print(serial_test)
```

```
##
##  Portmanteau Test (asymptotic)
##
## data:  Residuals of VAR object var_model
## Chi-squared = 75.875, df = 81, p-value = 0.6401
```

```
## $serial
##
##  Portmanteau Test (asymptotic)
##
## data:  Residuals of VAR object var_model
## Chi-squared = 75.875, df = 81, p-value = 0.6401
```

6

42

Appendix

```
cat("\nNormality Test:\n")
```

```
##
## Normality Test:
```

```
print(normality_test)
```

```
## $JB
##
##   JB-Test (multivariate)
##
## data:  Residuals of VAR object var_model
## Chi-squared = 64.481, df = 6, p-value = 5.505e-12
##
##
## $Skewness
##
##   Skewness only (multivariate)
##
## data:  Residuals of VAR object var_model
## Chi-squared = 11.524, df = 3, p-value = 0.009203
##
##
## $Kurtosis
##
##   Kurtosis only (multivariate)
##
## data:  Residuals of VAR object var_model
## Chi-squared = 52.957, df = 3, p-value = 1.873e-11
```

```
## $jb.mul
## $jb.mul$JB
##
##   JB-Test (multivariate)
##
## data:  Residuals of VAR object var_model
## Chi-squared = 64.481, df = 6, p-value = 5.505e-12
##
##
## $jb.mul$Skewness
##
##   Skewness only (multivariate)
##
## data:  Residuals of VAR object var_model
## Chi-squared = 11.524, df = 3, p-value = 0.009203
##
##
## $jb.mul$Kurtosis
##
##   Kurtosis only (multivariate)
##
## data:  Residuals of VAR object var_model
## Chi-squared = 52.957, df = 3, p-value = 1.873e-11
```

7

43

Appendix

```
# 9. IMPULSE RESPONSE ANALYSIS ------------------------------------------------

# Calculate IRFs with bootstrapped CIs
irf_results <- tryCatch({
  irf(var_model,
      n.ahead = 20,
      boot = TRUE,
      ci = 0.95,
      runs = 100)
}, error = function(e) {
  message("Bootstrapped IRF failed, using asymptotic approximation")
  irf(var_model, n.ahead = 20, boot = FALSE)
})

# Plot all IRFs
plot(irf_results)
```

Orthogonal Impulse Response from GDP

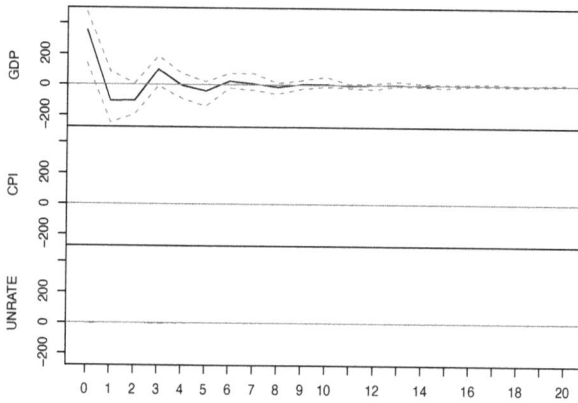

95 % Bootstrap CI, 100 runs

8

Appendix

Orthogonal Impulse Response from CPI

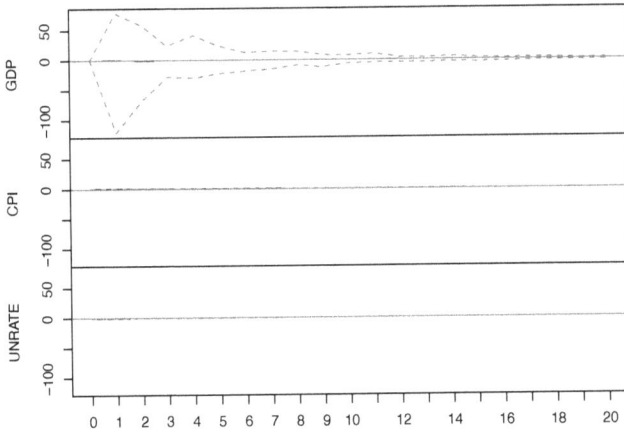

95 % Bootstrap CI, 100 runs

9

45

Appendix

Orthogonal Impulse Response from UNRATE

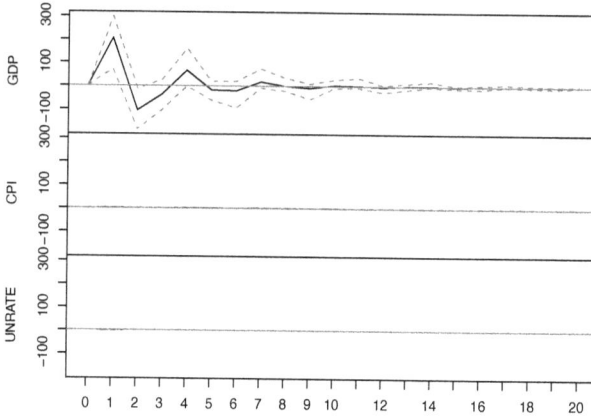

95 % Bootstrap CI, 100 runs

```
# 10. FORECAST ERROR VARIANCE DECOMPOSITION ----------------------------
perform_fevd_analysis <- function(var_model) {
  tryCatch({
    # Adaptive horizon based on sample size (fixed syntax)
    horizon <- min(8, floor(nrow(var_model$y)/4))  # Properly closed parentheses

    # Calculate FEVD
    message("Attempting FEVD with horizon = ", horizon)
    fevd_results <- fevd(var_model, n.ahead = horizon)

    # Process data
    response_var <- names(fevd_results)[1]
    plot_data <- as.data.frame(fevd_results[[response_var]]) %>%
      mutate(Horizon = 0:(nrow(.)-1)) %>%
      pivot_longer(-Horizon, names_to = "Shock", values_to = "Proportion")

    # Create plot
    ggplot(plot_data, aes(x = Horizon, y = Proportion, fill = Shock)) +
      geom_area(alpha = 0.7) +
      scale_fill_brewer(palette = "Set2") +
      labs(
        title = "Forecast Error Variance Decomposition",
        subtitle = paste("Decomposition of", response_var, "variance"),
        x = "Horizon (Quarters)",
        y = "Proportion Explained"
      ) +
```

10

46

Appendix

```r
    theme_minimal() +
    scale_y_continuous(labels = scales::percent_format(accuracy = 1))

  }, error = function(e) {
  message("FEVD analysis failed: ", e$message)
  return(NULL)
  })


}

# Generate FEVD plot
fevd_plot <- perform_fevd_analysis(var_model)
```

Attempting FEVD with horizon = 7

```r
# 11. FORECASTING ---------------------------------------------------------
perform_var_forecast <- function(var_model, economic_data, horizon = 8) {
  tryCatch({
    # Generate forecasts
    forecast_obj <- predict(var_model, n.ahead = horizon)

    # Prepare plot data for all variables
    forecast_data <- map_dfr(names(forecast_obj$fcst), function(var) {
      data.frame(
        date = seq(max(economic_data$date), by = "quarter", length.out = horizon + 1)[-1],
        value = forecast_obj$fcst[[var]][, "fcst"],
        lower = forecast_obj$fcst[[var]][, "lower"],
        upper = forecast_obj$fcst[[var]][, "upper"],
        variable = var
      )
    })

    # Create plot
    ggplot(forecast_data, aes(x = date, y = value)) +
      geom_ribbon(aes(ymin = lower, ymax = upper), alpha = 0.2, fill = "#1f77b4") +
      geom_line(color = "#1f77b4", linewidth = 1) +
      facet_wrap(~variable, scales = "free_y", ncol = 1) +
      labs(
        title = "VAR Model Forecast",
        x = "Date",
        y = "Value"
      ) +
      theme_minimal() +
      theme(panel.spacing = unit(1, "lines"))

  }, error = function(e) {
    message("Forecasting failed: ", e$message)
    return(NULL)
  })
}

# Generate forecast plot
```

11

47

Appendix

```r
forecast_plot <- perform_var_forecast(var_model, economic_data)

# 12. SAVE RESULTS --------------------------------------------------------
save_analysis_results <- function() {
  # Create plot list (only non-NULL plots)
  plots <- list(
    fevd = if(exists("fevd_plot")) fevd_plot else NULL,
    forecast = if(exists("forecast_plot")) forecast_plot else NULL,
    irf = if(exists("irf_results")) recordPlot(plot(irf_results)) else NULL
  )

  # Remove NULL elements
  plots <- plots[!sapply(plots, is.null)]

  # Save plots
  tryCatch({
    # Save as RDS for later reloading
    if(length(plots) > 0) {
      saveRDS(plots, "VAR_Plots.rds")
    }

    # Save individual PNG files
    if (!is.null(plots$fevd)) {
      ggsave("FEVD_Plot.png", plots$fevd, width = 10, height = 6, dpi = 300)
    }
    if (!is.null(plots$forecast)) {
      ggsave("Forecast_Plot.png", plots$forecast, width = 10, height = 8, dpi = 300)
    }
    if (!is.null(plots$irf)) {
      png("IRF_Plot.png", width = 1000, height = 800)
      replayPlot(plots$irf)
      dev.off()
    }

    message("Successfully saved ", length(plots), " plot(s)")
  }, error = function(e) {
    warning("Error saving plots: ", e$message)
  })

  # Save workspace
  save.image("VAR_Analysis_Final.RData")
}

# Execute saving
#save_analysis_results()
```

12

Bibliography

Alpaugh, Micah. "A Self-Defining Bourgeoisie in the Early French Revolution: The Milice Bourgeoise." *Journal of Social History* 47 (2014) 696–720. https://www.jstor.org/stable/43305956.

Antisemitism Awareness Act of 2025, S.558, 119th Cong. (2025–2026). https://www.congress.gov/bill/119th-congress/senate-bill/558.

Axelrod, Tal. "MAGA on 'Amnesty Watch' as Trump Weighs Migrant Worker Protections." Axios, July 10, 2025. https://www.axios.com/2025/07/10/trump-amnesty-illegal-immigration-workers.

Blake, John. "Putin Is Making the Same Mistakes That Doomed Hitler When He Invaded the Soviet Union." CNN, Apr. 2, 2022. https://www.cnn.com/2022/04/02/world/putin-invasion-mistakes-hitler-blake-cec.

Calhoun, Laurie. *Theodicy: A Metaphilosophical Investigation.* N.p.: Subversive Pulp, 2018.

Compston, Christine, and Rachel Seidman, eds. *Our Documents: 100 Milestone Documents from the National Archives.* Oxford: Oxford University Press, 2003.

Dobbin, Robert, trans. *Epictetus: Discourses and Select Writings.* New York: Penguin, 2008.

Dunford, Daniel, et al. "Coronavirus: The World in Lockdown in Maps and Charts." BBC, April 6, 2020. https://www.bbc.com/news/world-52103747.

Geoghegan, Tom, and James FitzGerald. "What Do We Know About the Epstein Files?" BBC, July 24, 2025. https://www.bbc.com/news/articles/c2or07dg6kro.

Gilderhus, Mark T. *History and Historians: A Hypsographical Introduction.* 7th ed. London: Pearson, 2010.

Hayek, F. A. *The Road to Serfdom.* Chicago: University of Chicago Press, 1944.

He, Elaine, and Lionel Laurent. "The World Is Masking Up, Some Are Opting Out." Bloomberg, July 16, 2020. https://www.bloomberg.com/graphics/2020-opinion-coronavirus-global-face-mask-adoption/.

International Court of Justice. *Application of the Convention on the Prevention and Punishment of Genocide in the Gaza Strip (South Africa v. Israel), Order of 5 April 2024.* https://www.icj-cij.org/sites/default/files/case-related/192/192-20240405-ord-01-00-en.pdf.

International Criminal Court. "State of Palestine." Information for Victims, Mar. 7, 2023. https://www.icc-cpi.int/victims/state-palestine.

Kashin, Vasily. "Behind the Illusion of Deadlock: What's Really Happening in the Ukraine Conflict." RT, Oct. 7, 2025. https://www.rt.com/russia/626032-war-west-cant-win/.

Kates, Steven. "Why Keynesian Concepts Cannot Be Used to Explain Pre-Keynesian Economic Thought: A Reader's Guide to Classical Theory." *Quarterly Journal of Austrian Economics* 17 (2014) 313-26.

Loria, Francesca, et al. "Economic Theories and Macroeconomic Reality." *Journal of Monetary Economics* 126 (2022) 105–17. https://doi.org/10.1016/j.jmoneco.2021.12.001.

Majaski, Christina. "Output Gap: What It Means, Pros & Cons of Using It, and Example." Investopedia, Aug. 12, 2024, https://www.investopedia.com/terms/o/outputgap.asp.

McKeon, Richard, ed. *Basic Works of Aristotle.* Chapel Hill: University of North Carolina Press, 2001.

Mises, Ludwig von. "Lord Keynes and Say's Law of Markets: The Contribution of Each to the Theory of the Trade Cycle." *The Freeman* 1 (1950) 83–85.

Paine, Thomas. *Common Sense.* New York: Penguin Classics, 1986.

Pipes, Richard. *A Concise History of the Russian Revolution.* New York: Vintage, 1996.

RT. "Russia–Ukraine Conflict." https://www.rt.com/trends/russia-ukraine-conflict/.

Say, Jean-Baptiste. *A Treatise on Political Economy.* Cosimo Classics, 2007. Originally published in 1803.

Stanley-Smith, Joe. "19 EU Countries Condemn Israel's 'Restrictive' Aid Rules in Gaza." Politico, Aug. 12, 2025. https://www.politico.eu/article/eu-countries-condemn-israel-humanitarian-aid-war-in-gaza-starvation-famine/.

Steele, Joel. *Philosophy of Qohelet: A Critical Analysis of Existentialism.* Eugene, OR: Wipf & Stock, 2021.

———. *Philosophy of War: A Brief Analysis of Principles and Justifications.* Eugene, OR: Wipf & Stock, 2020.

Takala, Rudy. "H-1Bs Are Wreaking Havoc on American Workers." The Hill, Aug. 11, 2025. https://thehill.com/opinion/immigration/5443667-h-1bs-are-wreaking-havoc-on-american-workers/.

Victor, Jacob M. "Regulating Sexual Orientation Change Efforts: The California Approach, Its Limitations, and Potential Alternatives." *The Yale Law Journal* 123 (2014) https://www.yalelawjournal.org/note/regulating-sexual-orientation-change-efforts-the-california-approach-its-limitations-and-potential-alternatives.

Bibliography

Vine, Davide. "Where in the World Is the U.S. Military?" Politico Magazine, July/Aug., 2015. https://www.politico.com/magazine/story/2015/06/us-military-bases-around-the-world-119321/.

Wermenbol, Grace. "The Post-October 7 Specter of the Holocaust." Georgetown Journal of International Affairs, Jan. 22, 2025. https://gjia.georgetown.edu/2025/01/22/the-post-october-7-specter-of-the-holocaust/.

www.ingramcontent.com/pod-product-compliance
Lightning Source LLC
Chambersburg PA
CBHW070954280326
41934CB00009B/2068